P9-EJJ-413

GENE PERRET

RETIREMENT
Twice the Time
Half the Money

COVER ILLUSTRATION BY
JAMES R. SHEPHERD

FLIP-BOOK ILLUSTRATIONS BY
VICKY SNOW

*To Dowd,
Take time for
some laughs —
Best
Gene Perret*

WitWorks™

WitWorks™

a funny little division of arizona highways books

2039 West Lewis Avenue, Phoenix, Arizona 85009
Telephone: (602) 712-2200
Web site: www.witworksbooks.com

Publisher — Win Holden
Managing Editor — Bob Albano
Associate Editor — Evelyn Howell
Associate Editor — P. K. McMahon
Art Director — Mary Winkelman Velgos
Photography Director — Peter Ensenberger
Production Director — Cindy Mackey

Copyright © 2001, Arizona Department of Transportation.

WitWorks™ is a trademark
of the Arizona Department of Transportation,
parent of *Arizona Highways*.

All rights reserved. Except for quotations used in articles, reviews,
and listings concerning this book, no part of this
book may be reproduced in any form by any means,
including photocopying, recording, or information storage
and retrieval system, without written permission
from the publisher.

Library of Congress Catalog Number: 00-110194
ISBN 1-893860-26-4

RETIREMENT: Twice the Time, Half the Money
FIRST EDITION, published in 2001.
Printed in the United States.

Book designer — Mary Winkelman Velgos

RETIREMENT:

That's when you return
from work one day and
say, "Hi, Honey, I'm home
— forever."

And she says to herself:
"Now I have something
else around the house
that has to be dusted."

And either one can say:
"I married you for better
or for worse and
retirement with you is
all of that."

ONE NICE THING ABOUT
RETIREMENT IS YOU CAN GET
OUT OF BED ANYTIME OF
THE DAY YOU LIKE . . .
AND AS OFTEN AS YOU LIKE.
AND ONCE YOU GET UP,
YOU CAN TAKE THE REST OF
THE DAY OFF.

*Another nice thing
is all the discounts
retirees get.
If I had known that,
I would have
gotten older sooner.*

Actually, not all discounts
are good. As a retiree
I get in to see the movies
for 10 percent less.
I'd rather pay full
price and have them
make the movies
10 percent better.

MORE AND MORE PEOPLE

ARE RETIRING AND FISHING,

FISHING, FISHING.

IT'S A GREAT TIME TO BE

ALIVE . . . UNLESS YOU'RE A

BAIT WORM.

Have you heard the Retiree's Credo? Anything that's worth doing is worth doing in a golf cart.

I know one guy
who doesn't want
to retire because
he would miss the
two weeks vacation.

RETIREMENT

IS NATURE'S WAY

OF SAYING,

"SO WHAT D'YA

WANNA DO NOW?"

*My husband
promised we'd travel
when he retired,
and we do . . . back and
forth to the
community center.*

*How come when
my husband does
absolutely nothing,
I still have to
clean up after
he does it?*

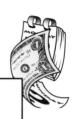

RETIREMENT IS

WONDERFUL.

IT'S DOING NOTHING

WITHOUT WORRYING

ABOUT GETTING

CAUGHT AT IT.

One question
I have about
retirement — who
OKs my expense
vouchers?

*Retirement does
not necessarily
mean inactivity.
Only if you're
doing it right.*

Retirement is a
great time to learn
to do something new —
like nothing.

Now that I'm retired,
people keep telling me
to do something.
That's the same thing my
boss used to tell me
when I was working.

ALL WORK AND NO PLAY

MAKE JACK

A DULL BOY.

ALL PLAY AND

NO WORK MAKE FOR A

GREAT RETIREMENT.

*If I had known
that getting paid
for doing nothing
was this much fun,
I would have gone
into politics.*

To some, the drawback
of retirement is that
it's boring.
To others, the appeal
of retirement is that
it's boring.

Our local theater offers a 10 percent discount to retirees. That's not that much when you consider I'm 100 percent retired.

I'M RETIRED!

WAKE ME WHEN

MY SOCIAL SECURITY

CHECK COMES.

I'm enjoying retirement
because I have a
nice little nest egg.
My wife would have
preferred a house.

*We retirees live
on a fixed income.
That means everything
we have has been fixed
because we can't afford
to buy anything new.*

Now that I'm retired,
I can do all the things
I've always wanted
to do . . . right after
I finish all the things
my wife has been
after me for years
to get done.

THE FIRST THING I DID

ON MY RETIREMENT

WAS TRAVEL.

I TOOK MY ALARM CLOCK

TO THE DUMP.

*Retirement has
no deadlines.
You've got
nothing to do.
If you get nothing
done today, you
can do it tomorrow.*

Retirement means
no pressure, no stress,
no heartache . . . unless
you play golf.

WHEN YOU RETIRE, YOU

SWITCH BOSSES — FROM

THE ONE WHO HIRED YOU

TO THE ONE

WHO MARRIED YOU.

RETIREMENT IS WHEN YOU

CAN KEEP

PUTTING OFF

FOR YEARS ALL

THOSE THINGS YOU'VE

BEEN PUTTING OFF

FOR YEARS.

They gave me a gold watch when I retired, so now I always know exactly what time I don't have to be at work.

At my retirement,
the boss said they wanted
to give me something I've
had my eye on for years,
but his secretary
still has 30 years to go
to her retirement.

I told the boss that
during my retirement
I plan to be more active
than I've ever been.
He said, "I imagine you
would have to be."

YOU KNOW THOSE THINGS

YOU'VE ALWAYS WANTED

TO DO?

WELL, RETIREMENT

IS A WONDERFUL TIME TO

SIT AROUND

AND WONDER WHY YOU

EVER WANTED

TO DO THEM.

You're really doing your retirement right if the family dog is jealous of you.

RETIREMENT IS SIMPLE.

MY APPOINTMENT BOOK

HAS BEEN REPLACED BY

AN INDEX CARD.

It used to be
"another day,
another dollar."
Now it's "another week,
another prescription
filled."

Retirement's funny.
Now that I can
stay home all day
they give me a discount
to ride the buses.

YESTERDAY WAS HECTIC.

MY TEE TIME

WAS CHANGED.

I now consider myself
an active senior.
The remote control
for my TV set
is broken.

*I am wallowing
in retirement.
I have goldfish
at home who are
busier than I am.
I do absolutely nothing,
but on my own time.*

The worst part of doing

nothing all day is that

tomorrow . . . you've got

to do it

all over again.

HAVE SOME HOBBIES

WHEN YOU'RE RETIRED.

IT'S ALWAYS GOOD TO

HAVE SOMETHING

TO PUT OFF UNTIL

TOMORROW.

I can get into museums
now on a discount.
That's only fair since
I'm older than
most of the exhibits.

I LOVE RETIREMENT.

IT WOULD HAVE BEEN

A NICE WAY TO

SPEND MY YOUTH.

NOW THAT I'M IN MY

LATER YEARS I DON'T

PAY FULL PRICE FOR

ANYTHING . . . EXCEPT

MY EARLIER YEARS.

*Even when I go to
the Free Library
I ask for the
senior citizen discount.*

At 62 I'm paying the
same price as
children under 12.
That pleases some
retirees. Not me.
I'm upset about the
50 years I've been
overcharged.

RETIREMENT IS BEING

UNTROUBLED, CAREFREE,

FUN-LOVING.

IT'S KIND OF LIKE COLLEGE

DAYS WITHOUT THE

STUDIES.

I NO LONGER

HAVE TO WORK

FOR A LIVING

SO I PLAY GOLF.

SAME THING.

I enjoy waking up
and not having
to go to work.
So I do it
three or four
times a day.

I work harder at
my retirement than
I ever worked
at my job.
Which gives you
some idea why
my co-workers
weren't terribly upset
to see me go.

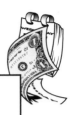

RETIREMENT DOES NOT

MEAN DOING ABSOLUTELY

NOTHING. BUT ON ANY

GIVEN DAY, IT CAN.

*I've left my mark in the
business world.
Now I just leave divots
all over
the golf course.*

I'VE BEEN DOING NOTHING

FOR ABOUT

FIVE YEARS NOW.

AND NEXT MONTH

I RETIRE.

I accomplished
everything I wanted to
in my career
before retiring — with
the possible exception
of learning how
to use the office
copier machine.

Retirement means
that now you leave
coffee cup rings
on your own
furniture.

MY RETIREMENT PARTY WAS

GREAT FUN.

IT'S KIND OF DISTRESSING

TO SEE THAT MANY PEOPLE

SO HAPPY

TO SEE YOU GO.

In my retirement
I do a lot of fishing,
hunting, and hiking
through the woods.
It's called "golf."

My spouse says

she married me

for better or

for worse.

Then she adds,

"When you went

to work every day, that

was better."

IN MY RETIREMENT,

I HAVE AN EASY CHAIR

THAT NO ONE ELSE

EVER SITS IN.

THAT'S BECAUSE I'M

ALWAYS IN IT.

My spouse still serves me
three square meals a day.
She says they match
my personality since
I've retired.

I went from being low man in the company hierarchy to being a full-time husband. It's a lateral move.

In my retirement I go

for a short swim at

least once or twice

every day.

It's either that or

buy a new golf ball.

*We had a great turnout at
my retirement party.
As my boss said, "When
you give the people what
they want . . . "*

Retirement: It's nice to get out of the rat race, but you have to learn to get along with less cheese.

THERE WERE

SO MANY THINGS

I WANTED TO DO WHEN

I RETIRED BUT

I'VE EITHER FORGOTTEN

WHAT THEY WERE OR

HOW TO DO THEM.

Doing nothing is so much fun I'm sorry I wasted so many years doing something.

Some folks love
retirement and
others hate it.
The latter are
usually married
to the retirees.

Retirement is when you finally get a chance to do the things you want to do . . . unless you're married.

I'LL PROBABLY

BE RETIRED

FOR THE REST OF MY LIFE

— IF NOT LONGER.

Someday I have to fix
the toaster, the clock-
radio, the VCR . . . but
I keep putting it off.
I don't want to be the
only thing around the
house that's not
working.

I said at my
retirement dinner,
"I'm anxious to see what
it's like to get paid for
doing nothing."
My boss said,
"I would think you'd
know by now."

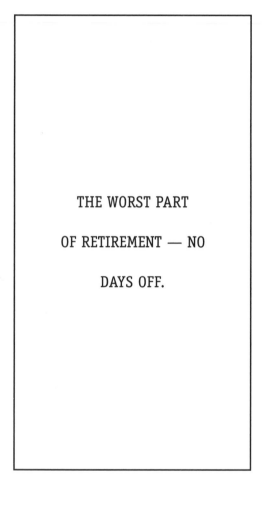

THE WORST PART

OF RETIREMENT — NO

DAYS OFF.

I got a set of luggage
as a retirement gift.
These people
not only wanted me
out of the office,
but out of the state.

I go for a long walk every day during my retirement. It reminds me of my old company parking space.

Even though I'm retired now, the sun still comes up every morning and sets every night — and I'm never awake to see either one of them.

Anyone who thinks
retirement is the
"easy life" has never
seen the amount
of work that's waiting
to be done around
my house.

The good part of
retirement
is that you become
your own boss.
The bad part is you
notice that management
has not improved.

WHY RETIRE

AND DO NOTHING?

FOR THAT YOU

COULD HAVE

STAYED AT WORK.

You can travel all you want when you're retired. Just keep in mind that you're paying for your own expense account.

One restaurant I know

never gives a senior

citizen discount.

Their philosophy is:

If you remember

to ask for it, you're

not old enough

to get it.

BEFORE I RETIRED

I USED TO LOOK FORWARD

TO FRIDAYS.

NOW I HAVE TROUBLE

REMEMBERING WHICH

DAY OF THE WEEK IT IS.

I'VE BECOME AN

OUTDOOR PERSON IN

MY RETIREMENT.

THAT'S WHERE

THE HAMMOCK IS.

If you're not loafing

in your retirement,

you're not working

hard enough at it.

Retirement works out
nicely. You get to
do nothing
at about the same time
your doctor says that's all
you're allowed to do.

WHEN YOU RETIRE

YOU CAN DO ANYTHING

YOU WANT TO DO.

THE SECRET IS NOT TO

WANT TO DO ANYTHING.

A diligent retiree says
never put off till
tomorrow what you can
forget about altogether.

IF THIS IS WHAT

I WORKED SO HARD FOR,

I COULD'VE

TAKEN IT

A LOT EASIER.

When I was younger
I didn't have the time.
Now that I've got the
time, I don't have the
wherewithal.

WHAT DOES A RETIREE

DO FOR A LIVING?

HE LIVES.

I worked so hard to get
out of my job that now
I have trouble getting
out of my chair.

Retirement comes too late. I've already lost interest in the things I've always been interested in.

Be prudent in your
retirement.
Realize you're
no longer able to do
the things you've
always wanted to do.

MY GREAT-GREAT

GRANDFATHER

NEVER RETIRED.

THAT'S BECAUSE HE WAS AN

OLD INDIAN FIGHTER. AND

GREAT-GREAT GRANDMOM

WAS AN OLD INDIAN.

Life is mean.

When I was working,

I hated getting up at

6 A.M. to go to work. Now

that I'm retired,

I wake up at 5.

There's one bad thing
about retirement — days
seem longer when you
don't have quitting time
to look forward to.

RETIREE: HI, HONEY,
I'M HOME.

SPOUSE: STILL?

I always thought I knew

what I wanted to do

when I retired.

Now I have to check

with my doctor.

I'M NOW AS FREE AS THE

BREEZE — WITH ROUGHLY

THE SAME INCOME.

As a retiree I have
no obligations or
responsibilities.
I feel like a rainspout
on a sunny day.

*In retirement, you'll find
that you can't teach an
old dog new tricks.
In fact, some of the old
tricks become rather
painful, too.*

My wife doesn't mind
having me around
the house
all the time.
In fact, in my loose
fitting shorts, sloppy
T-shirt, floppy hat, and
comfortable shoes,
she'd rather
I not be seen out
in public.

I'VE MADE MY

CONTRIBUTIONS TO THE

BUSINESS WORLD.

NOW I'M CONTENT TO LEAVE

IT TO YOUNGER FOLKS TO

REPAIR THE DAMAGE.

Retirement is not
for sissies.
Only us older folks
are strong enough
to endure it.

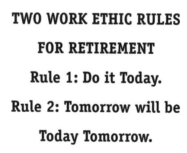

TWO WORK ETHIC RULES

FOR RETIREMENT

Rule 1: Do it Today.

Rule 2: Tomorrow will be

Today Tomorrow.

I LOVE DOING NOTHING.

IT GIVES ME A SENSE

OF ACCOMPLISHMENT.

I used to roll up my
sleeves and go to work
each morning.
Now I roll up my sleeve
once a year
to get my flu shot.

The boss said no one
could ever replace me
but with the amount of
work I've been doing
lately,
no one would have to.

AFTER TWO WEEKS OF

RETIREMENT MY WIFE

IS AFTER ME TO TAKE UP

A HOBBY — LIKE

ENLISTING IN THE ARMY.

I sleep like a baby
at night.
All those naps
during the day
seem to tire me out.

I was a fixture for years
at the office.
Now they're eager
to replace me
with a worker.

*I used to carry
a lot of weight
around the office,
but that's all
behind me now.*

EVEN THOUGH I'M RETIRED,

I PLAN MY DAY

EVERY MORNING.

I TAKE A BLANK SHEET

OF PAPER AND

LEAVE IT LIKE THAT.

*Now that we have more
time together, my wife
and I enjoy competitive
activities — like fighting
over who controls
the thermostat.*

Of all the bad habits
I've ever broken,
working for a living
was the most rewarding.

I DO MAINTAIN A HEALTHY

EXERCISE PROGRAM IN MY

RETIREMENT.

I TAKE AT LEAST

TWO BRISK NAPS A DAY.

I WORK ON

A FEW SMALL PROJECTS

AROUND THE HOUSE.

MY WIFE WON'T LET ME

NEAR THE BIG ONES.

Both me and the family
dog do absolutely nothing
around the house all day.
She can't figure out why
I'm allowed to eat at
the table.

My wife always
enjoyed having
little knickknacks
around the house.
Now I've become one.

*The boss said at my
going away party,
"Retiring doesn't mean
you're no longer useful —
just not to us."*

RACEHORSES RETIRE

TO STUD.

I HAVE NO IDEA WHY

I CHOSE GARDENING.

In my retirement
I like to do things
with my hands — like
turn off the
alarm clock.

I like to make things and
give them to my
children. I'm getting
even for all those
ashtrays they made me
in metal shop.

LEISURE:

A FANCY WORD

FOR PEOPLE

WHO DON'T WANT

TO ADMIT

THEY'RE BORED.

A RETIREE'S BIGGEST FIB:

"HOLD ON.

I'LL CHECK MY

SCHEDULE."

I enjoy retirement.
I was pretty doggone
good at my work, but I'm
no slouch at doing
nothing, either.

I keep busy in my
retirement — struggling
with the family dog
for the best spot
on the sofa.

The best part of doing
nothing is that there's
no way to do it wrong.

*Every morning my wife
asks me, "What are you
going to do today?"
And then we both
laugh . . .*

MY WIFE HAS BEEN LOOKING

FOR IDEAS THAT WOULD

GET ME OUT OF THE HOUSE

MORE. SHE FINALLY DECIDED

ON A COURT ORDER.

I don't know why
I've become a
cantankerous, old retiree.
Before I was just
a cantankerous,
old working person.

According to my spouse,
retirement means going
from overworked to
underfoot.

On the day of my
retirement
I told my spouse,
"I'm home for good."
She said, "You're home.
The 'good' part
remains to be seen."

Before retirement I used
to come home and say,
"What's for dinner?"
Now I stay home and say,
"What's for breakfast?"
"What's for lunch?" and
"What's for dinner?"

SOME RESTAURANTS HAVE

REDUCED PRICES FOR

RETIREES.

I DON'T KNOW WHY.

I ENJOY EATING JUST AS

MUCH AS WHEN

I WAS WORKING.

*I'm officially
retired now. My wife
turned my briefcase
into a planter.*

MY WIFE AND I

TOOK UP GOLF SO WE'D

HAVE SOMETHING

TO DO TOGETHER,

BUT IT DIDN'T WORK.

SHE SLICES AND I HOOK.

Retirement can be
educational.
Since I've been around
the house, my wife says
she's learned why my boss
was such a grouch.

I said to my wife,
"What can I do to help
around the house?"
She said, "Ask for
your old job back."

MAN SHOULD EARN HIS

BREAD BY THE SWEAT OF

HIS BROW.

AND RETIREMENT IS A

GREAT ANTIPERSPIRANT.

RETIREMENT IS LIKE A

SECOND CHILDHOOD.

MY WIFE SAYS THINGS TO

ME NOW THAT SHE USED

TO SAY TO THE KIDS.

I said to my wife,
"Why did you buy me a
fishing rod for my
retirement?
The nearest lake is
100 miles away."
She said, "You answered
your own question."

Other Funny Little Books From **WitWorks**

**Cow Pie Ain't No Dish
You Take to the County Fair**
Cartoonist Jim Willoughby
and a team of writers churn
up fun with their version of
cowboys' facts of life.
$6.95   #ACWP7

**Never Give a Heifer
a Bum Steer**
Arizona's official historian
Marshall Trimble bases his
jokes and tall tales on the folks
he grew up with in Ash Fork.
$7.95   #ANVP9

**Growing Older is
So Much Fun
EVERYBODY'S Doing It**
Gene Perret delivers a spate of
one-liners that cast a funny
glow over senior citizenship.
$6.95   #AGOP0

**Someday I Want to Go
to All the Places
My Luggage Has Been**
Gene Perret's brief essays
poke fun at the things about
travel that bug us.
$7.95   #ALLP9

**Never Stand Between a
Cowboy and His Spittoon**
Here's a gross of jokes taken
from newspapers published
before Arizona became a state
in 1912. Some are classy.
Others are crass. But all are a
historical reflection of what
was funny at the time.
$6.95   #ABLP0

Do You Pray, Duke?
Cowboy-oriented chuckles
from cartoonist Jim
Willoughby.
$6.95   #ADDP0

*For Release in
September 2001:*

**Grandchildren Are
So Much Fun We Should
Have Had Them First**
Gene Perret's witticisms
speak to grandparents
everywhere.
$6.95   #AGRS3

*available
in bookstores*

To order a book or request a catalog from WitWorks™
call toll-free **1-800-543-5432**.
In Phoenix or outside the U.S., call **602-712-2000**.
Online at **www.witworksbooks.com**